SCOTTISH
SONGS

D0496284

SCOTTISH
SONGS

WAVERLEY BOOKS

Published 2010 by Waverley Books,
144 Port Dundas Road, Glasgow, G4 0HZ

© Copyright 2003 Geddes & Grosset
The edition first published 2009, reprinted 2010

Compiled in part by RLS Ltd, 1998
with further selections by Mairi Campbell, 2003

Music typesetting by Neil Gowans, 1998 and
Chalmers Enterprises, Edinburgh, 2003

Musical arrangements for the 2003 edition by Margaret Christie

'Scotland the Brave' © Copyright the estate of Cliff Hanley and
reproduced with the kind permission of the Hanley family

'Flower of Scotland' © Copyright The Corries (Music) Ltd
and reproduced with permission.
Arrangement by Margaret Christie, 2004.

ISBN 978 1 902407 88 3

Printed and bound in the UK

Contents

Contents

SCOTTISH
SONGS

Ae Fond Kiss

Ae fond kiss, and then we sev - er! Ae fare - weel, and

D   G   D   A Bmin   G

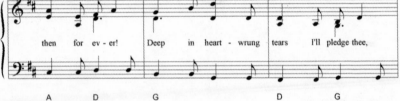

then for ev - er! Deep in heart - wrung tears I'll pledge thee,

A   D   G   D   G

War - ring sighs and groans I'll wage thee.

D   A7 D   G   D   A   D

Who shall say that Fortune grieves him,
While the star of hope she leaves him?
Me, nae cheerful twinkle lights me,
Dark despair around benights me.

I'll ne'er blame my partial fancy,
Naething could resist my Nancy;
But to see her was to love her,
Love but her, and love for ever.

Had we never loved sae kindly,
Had we never loved sae blindly,
Never met, or never parted,
We had ne'er been broken-hearted!

Fare thee weel, thou first and fairest,
Fare thee weel, thou best and dearest;
Thine be ilka joy and treasure,
Peace, enjoyment, love, and pleasure!

Ae fond kiss, and then we sever!
Ae fareweel, alas! For ever!
Deep in heart-wrung tears I'll pledge thee,
Warring sighs and groans I'll wage thee.

Robert Burns

Annie Laurie

Her brow is like the snaw-drift,
Her neck is like the swan;
Her face it is the fairest
That e'er the sun shone on.
That e'er the sun shone on,
And dark-blue is her e'e;
And for bonnie Annie Laurie
I'd lay me doun and dee.

Like dew on the gowan lying
Is the fa' o' her fairy feet;
And like winds in summer sighing,
Her voice is low and sweet.
Her voice is low and sweet,
And she's a' the world to me;
And for bonnie Annie Laurie
I'd lay me doun and dee.

William Douglas

As I Gaed Doun Glenmoriston

As I gaed doun Glen - mo - ris - ton, Where wa - ters meet a - bout Al-

tee - rie, I saw my las - sie mil - kin' kye Wi'

skil - fu' hand and sang sae chee - rie. The wind that stirred her

gow - den hair Blew saft - ly frae the hill at ev - en, And

like a moor - land flower she looked That licht - ly lifts its head to hea - ven.

Frae that sweet hour her name I'd breathe
Wi' nocht but clouds and hills to hear me,
And when the warld to rest was laid
I'd watch for dawn and wish her near me,
Till ane by ane the stars were gane,
The moor-cock to his mate called clearly,
And daylicht glinted on the burn
Where red-deer cross at mornin' early.

The years are lang, the wark is sair,
And life is aftimes wae and wearie,
Yet Foyer's flood shall cease to fall
Ere my love fail unto my dearie.
I lo'ed her then, I lo'e her now,
And cauld the warld wad be without her,
The croodlin' bairnies at her knee
And licht o' mither's love about her.

Harold Boulton

Auld Lang Syne

Should auld ac-quaint-ance be for-got, And nev-er brought to mind? Should auld ac-quaint-ance be for-got, And days o' lang— syne? For auld lang - syne my dear, For auld lang - syne; We'll tak' a cup o' kind - ness yet, For auld lang - syne.

We twa ha'e run aboot the braes,
And pu'd the gowans fine,
But we've wandered mony a weary foot
Sin' auld lang syne.

For auld lang syne, my dear,
For auld lang syne;
We'll tak a cup o' kindness yet,
For auld lang syne.

We twa ha'e paidl't in the burn
Frae morning sun till dine;
But seas between us braid ha'e roared
Sin' auld lang syne.

For auld, etc.

And surely I'll be your pint-stoup,
And surely you'll be mine;
And we'll tak' a cup o' kindness yet,
For auld lang syne.

For auld, etc.

And here's a hand, my trusty fiere,
And gie's a hand o' thine;
And we'll tak' a richt gude willie-waucht
For auld lang syne.

For auld, etc.

Robert Burns

Aye Waukin' O!

When first she cam' to our toun
They ca'd her Grace Macfarlane,
But now she's gane awa'
They ca' her a' folks' darlin';

Aye waukin' O!
Waukin' aye and weary,
Sleep I can get nane
For thinkin' o' my dearie;
Aye waukin' O!

When I sleep I dream,
When I wake I'm eerie,
Rest I can get nane
For thinkin' o' my dearie;

Aye waukin' O! etc.

Lanely nicht comes on,
A' the lave are sleepin',
I think upon my bonnie lass
And bleer my e'en wi' greetin'.

Aye waukin' O! etc.

Her minnie lo'es her weel,
Her daddie lo'es her better,
And I lo'e the lass mysel',
Wae's me I canna get her;

Aye waukin' O! etc.

Old Scottish Song

The Barnyards o' Delgaty

In New Deer par-ish I was born, A child of youth to
G *C* *G*

Meth-lick came; And gin' ye'll no be-lieve my word the sess-ion clerk will
C *D* *G* *C* *G* *Bmin*

Chorus
tell the same. Lin-ten ad-ie, toor-in ad-ie, Lin-ten ad-ie,
Emin *G* *Bmin* *G*

toor-in ae; Lin-ten, lour-in, lin-ten, lour-in,
C *D* *G* *Cmaj7*

Lin-ten lour-in, lour-in lee.
G *D* *G*

As I cam' in by Netherdale,
At Turra market for to fee,
I fell in wi' a farmer chiel
Fae the barnyards o' Delgaty.

Linten addie, toorin addie,
Linten addie, toorin ae;
Linten, lourin, linten, lourin,
Linten, lourin, lourin, lee.

He promised me the ae best pair
That e'er I set my een upon:
When I gaed hame tae Barnyards
There was naethin there but skin and bone.

Linten addie, etc.

The auld black horse sat on his rump;
The auld grey mear lay on her wime:
For a' that I could hup and crack
They wouldna rise at yokin' time.

Linten addie, etc.

I can drink and nae be drunk;
I can fecht and nae be slain;
I can kiss another's lass,
And aye be welcome tae my ain.

Linten addie, etc.

My can'le noo it is brunt oot:
The snotter's fairly on the wane;
Sae fare ye weel, ye barnyards -
Ye'll never catch me here again.

Linten addie, etc.

The Blue Bell of Scotland

Oh where, and oh where, did your Highland laddie dwell?
Oh where, and oh where, did your Highland laddie dwell?
He dwelt in merry Scotland, where grows the sweet blue bell,
And it's oh! in my heart I love the laddie well.

Oh what, and oh what, does your Highland laddie wear?
Oh what, and oh what, does your Highland laddie wear?
He wears the plaided tartan around his form so fair;
And it's oh! in my heart I wish that he were here.

Blue Bonnets Over the Border

Chorus

March! March! Et-trick and Te-vi-ot-dale! Why, my lads, din-na ye march for-ward in or - der? March! March! Esk-dale and Lid-des-dale, All the Blue Bon-nets are o - ver the bor - der! Ma - ny a ban-ner spread, Flut-ters a-bove your head, Ma - ny a crest that is fa-mous in sto - ry! Mount and make rea-dy then, sons of the moun-tain glen, Fight for your King, and the old Scot-tish glo - ry.

March! March! Ettrick and Teviotdale!
Why, my lads, dinna ye march forward in order?
March! March! Eskdale and Liddesdale,
All the Blue Bonnets are over the Border!

Many a banner spread flutters above your head,
Many a crest that is famous in story!
Mount and make ready then, sons of the mountain glen,
Fight for your king, and the old Scottish glory.

Come from the hills where the hirsels are grazing,
Come from the glen of the buck and the roe;
Come to the crag where the beacon is blazing;
Come with the buckler, the lance and the bow.

Trumpets are sounding, war steeds are bounding,
Stand to your arms and march in good order.
England shall many a day talk of the bloody fray
When the Blue Bonnets came over the Border!

The Boatman

How of-ten hun-ting the high-est hill-top I scan the o-cean thy sail to

Emin   B   Amin

see; Wilt come to-night, love, wilt come to-mor-row, Or ev-er come love to com-fort

Emin   C   Emin   B

me? Fhir a bha-ta na ho-ro ei-le, Fhir a bha-ta na ho-ro ei-le, Fhir a

Emin   G   D   Emin   Bmin

bha-ta na ho-ro ei-le, O fare thee well, love where-e'r thou be.

C   G   Amin   B   Emin

They call thee fickle, they call thee false one,
And seek to change me, but all in vain;
No, thou'rt my dream yet throughout the dark night,
And every morn yet I watch the main.

Fhir a bhata, na horo eile,
Fhir a bhata, na horo eile,
Fhir a bhata, na horo eile,
O fare thee well, love, where e'er thou goest.

There's not a hamlet (too well I know it)
Where you go wandering or stay awhile,
But all its old folk you win with talking,
And charm its maidens with song and smile.

Fhir a bhata, etc.

Dost thou remember the promise made me,
The tartan plaidie, the silken gown,
The ring of gold with thy hair and portrait?
That gown and ring I will never own.

Fhir a bhata, etc.

Translated from the Gaelic by Thomas Pattison

Bonnie Dundee

To the Lords of Con-ven-tion 'twas Clav'r-house who spoke: "Ere the King's crown shall fall there are crowns to be broke, Then each cav-a-lier who loves hon-our and me, Let him fol-low the bon-net of Bon-nie Dun-dee." Come fill up my cup,— come fill up my can, Come sad-dle your hor-ses, and call out your men, Un-hook the West Port— and let us gae free, And it's

up wi' the bon-nets of Bon - nie Dun - dee.

E/B   B7   E

Dundee he is mounted, he rides up the street,
The bells are rung backward, the drums they are beat;
But the Provost, douce man, says "Just e'en let him be:
The toun is weel rid o' that de'il Dundee."

Come fill up my cup, come fill up my can,
Come saddle your horses, and call out your men,
Unhook the West Port, and let us gae free,
And it's up wi' the bonnets o' Bonnie Dundee.

"There are hills beyond Pentland, and lands beyond Forth;
Be there lords in the lowlands, they've chiefs in the north;
And brave dunie-wassals, three thousand times three,
Will cry Ho! for the bonnets of Bonnie Dundee.

Come fill up etc.

"Then away to the hills, to the caves, to the rocks:
Ere I own a usurper I'll couch with the fox;
And tremble, false Whigs, in the midst of your glee:
You have not seen the last of my bonnets and me."

Come fill up, etc.

Sir Walter Scott

The Bonnie Earl o' Moray

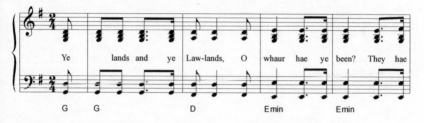

Ye lands and ye Law-lands, O whaur hae ye been? They hae

G G D Emin Emin

slain the Earl o' Mo - ray, and laid him on the green. He

C Amin Emin Emin G

was a braw gal-lant, and he rade at the ring; And the

G G Amin Amin

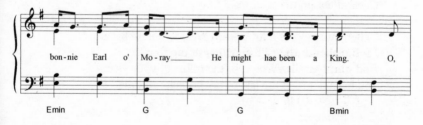

bon - nie Earl o' Mo - ray____ He might hae been a King. O,

Emin G G Bmin

O, wae betide ye, Huntly,
And wherefore did ye sae?
I bade ye bring him wi' you,
And forbad' ye him to slay.
He was a braw gallant,
And he played at the glove;
And the bonnie Earl o' Moray,
He was the Queen's love.
O, lang will his ladye look frae the Castle Doune
Ere she see the Earl o' Moray come soundin'
    through the toun.

Old Scottish Ballad

Bonnie Strathyre

Then there's mirth in the sheiling and love in my breast,
When the sun is gane doun and the kye are at rest;
For there's mony a prince wad be proud to aspire
To my winsome wee Maggie, the pride o' Strathyre.

Her lips are like rowans in ripe simmer seen,
And mild as the starlicht the glint o' her e'en;
Far sweeter her breath than the scent o' the briar,
And her voice is sweet music in bonnie Strathyre.

Set Flora by Colin, and Maggie by me,
And we'll dance to the pipes swellin' loudly and free,
Till the moon in the heavens climbing higher and higher
Bids us sleep on fresh brackens in bonnie Strathyre.

Though some to gay touns in the Lawlands will roam,
And some will gang sodgerin' far from their home;
Yet I'll aye herd my cattle, and bigg my ain byre,
And love my ain Maggie in bonnie Strathyre.

Harold Boulton

Bonnie Wee Thing

Bon - nie wee thing, can - ty wee thing, Love - ly wee thing,
wert thou mine; I would wear thee in my bo - som,
Lest my jew - el I should tine. Wist - ful - ly I
look and lan - guish, In that bon - nie face of thine; And my heart it
stounds with an - guish, Lest my wee thing be na mine.

Bonnie wee thing, canny wee thing,
Lovely wee thing, wert thou mine;
I would wear thee in my bosom,
Lest my jewel I should tine.

Wit and grace and love and beauty
In ae constellation shine!
To adore thee is my duty,
Goddess o' this soul o' mine.

Robert Burns

Brown-haired Maiden

Brown-haired maid-en, fresh and fair, Blithe and bright with light-some air,

Amin F C C F G C

Tues-day when I trys-ted thee All the week was worth to me.

C G G C Amin E Amin

Brown-haired maid with witching smile,
Full of love and free from guile,
Softly 'neath the hawthorn tree
Came thy whispered troth to me.

Young were we when first fond love
Found us in the hazel grove;
Sweet thy kisses were to me,
And thy voice was melody.

God be with thee, brown-haired maid,
In the sunshine or the shade;
Ev'ry Tuesday saved for thee
Brings a year of bliss to me.

***Translated from the Gaelic by
Professor Blackie***

The Bush Aboon Traquair

Will ye gang wi' me and fare To the bush a-boon Tra - quair? Owre the

C F C G C F G

high Minch - muir we'll up and a - wa', This

C Dmin C F Gsus4 G

bon - nie sim-mer noon, While the sun shines fair a - boon, And the

C F C G C F C

licht sklents saft - ly doun on holm and ha'. And the

C F F G C

And what wad ye do there,
At the bush aboon Traquair?
A lang dreich road, ye had better let it be;
Save some auld scrunts o' birk
I' the hill-side lirk,
There's nocht in the warld for man to see.

But the blythe lilt o' yon air,
The bush aboon Traquair,
I need nae mair, it's eneuch for me;
Owre my cradle its sweet chime
Cam' sughin' frae auld time,
Sae, tide what may be, I'll awa' and see.

And what saw ye there,
At the bush aboon Traquair?
Or what did ye hear that was worth your
  heed?
I heard the cushies croon
Thro' the gowden afternoon,
And the Quair burn singing doun to the vale
  o' Tweed.

And birks saw I three or four
Wi' grey moss bearded owre,
The last that are left o' the birken shaw,
Whar mony a simmer e'en
Fond lovers did convene,
Thae bonnie, bonnie gloamins that are lang
  awa'.

Frae mony a but and ben,
By muirland, holm, and glen,
They cam' ane hour to spen' on the green-
 wood swaird;
But lang ha'e lad an' lass
Been lying 'neath the grass,
The green, green grass o' Traquair kirkyard.

They were blest beyond compare
When they held their trysting there,
Amang thae greenest hills shone on by the
 sun;
And then they wan a rest,
The lownest and the best,
I' Traquair kirkyard when a' was dune.

Now the birks to dust may rot,
Names o' lovers be forgot,
Nae lads and lasses there ony mair convene,
But the blythe lilt o' yon air
Keeps the bush aboon Traquair
And the luve that ance was there aye fresh and
 green.

Principal Shairp

Ca' the Yowes to the Knowes

Ca' the yowes to the knowes, Ca' them whar the hea- ther grows,

Ca' them whar the burn - ie rowes, My bon - nie dear - ie. As

I gaed down the wa - ter side, There I met my shep- herd lad, He

row'd me sweet- ly in his plaid, And ca'd me his dear - ie.

'Will ye gang down the water-side,
And see the waves sae sweetly glide
Beneath the hazels spreading wide,
The moon it shines fu' clearly?'

Ca' the yowes to the knowes,
Ca' them them whar the heather grows,
Ca' them whar the burnie rows,
My bonnie dearie!

'I was bred up in nae sic school,
My shepherd lad, to play the fool,
An' a' the day to sit in dool,
An' naebody to see me.'

Ca' the yowes, etc.

'Ye sall get gowns and ribbons meet,
Cauf-leather shoon upon your feet,
And in my arms ye'se lie and sleep,
An' ye sall be my dearie.'

Ca' the yowes, etc.

'If ye'll but stand to what you've said,
I'se gang with you, my shepherd lad,
And ye may row me in your plaid,
And I sall be your dearie.'

Ca' the yowes, etc.

'While waters wimple to the sea,
While day blinks in the lift sae hie,
Till clae-cauld death sall blin' my e'e,
Ye sall be my dearie.'

Robert Burns

Caller Herrin'

Wha'll buy cal-ler her-rin'? They're bon-nie fish and hale-some fa-rin':

Buy my cal-ler her-rin', New drawn frae the Forth! When

ye were sleep-in' on your pil-lows, Dreamed ye aught o' our puir fel-lows,

Dark-ling as they face the bil-lows, A' to fill our wo-ven wil-lows?

Chorus

Buy my cal-ler her-rin', They're bon-nie fish and hale-some fa-rin';

Buy my cal-ler her-rin', New drawn frae the Forth.

G D Emin G D7 G

And when the creel o' herrin' passes,
Ladies, clad in silks and laces
Gather in their braw pelisses,
Toss their heads and screw their faces.
Buy my caller herrin'
New drawn frae the Forth.

Buy my caller herrin'?
They're bonnie fish and halesome fairin:
Buy my caller herrin',
New drawn frae the Forth!

Gude caller herrin's no got lightlie,
Ye can trip the spring fu' tightlie,
Spite o' tauntin', flauntin', flingin',
Gow has set you a' a-singin.
Buy my caller herrin'
New drawn frae the Forth.

Buy my etc.

But neebour wives, now tent my tellin',
When the bonny fish ye're sellin':
At ae word be aye your dealin' -
Truth will stan' when a'thing's failin'.
Buy my caller herrin'
New drawn frae the Forth.

Buy my etc.

Lady Nairne

The Campbells are Comin'

The great Argyle he goes before,
He makes the cannons and guns to roar,
Wi' sound o' trumpet, pipe and drum,
The Campbells are coming, oho, oho!

The Campbells are comin', oho, oho!
The Campbells are comin' oho, oho!
The Campbells are comin', to bonnie Loch Leven,
The Campbells are comin', oho, oho!

The Campbells they are a' in arms,
Their loyal faith and trust to show,
Wi' banners rattlin' in the wind
The Campbells are coming, oho, oho!

The Campbells are coming, etc.

Charlie Is My Darling

As he cam' marching up the street,
The pipes play'd loud and clear,
And a' the folk cam' runnin' out
To see the Chevalier.

Oh! Charlie is my darling,
My darling, my darling,
Oh! Charlie is my darling,
The young Chevalier.

Wi' hieland bonnets on their heads
And claymores bright and clear,
They've cam' to fight for Scotland's right
And the young Chevalier.

Oh! Charlie, etc.

They've left their bonnie hieland hills,
Their wives and bairnies dear,
To draw the sword for Scotland's lord:
The young Chevalier.

Oh! Charlie etc.

Oh, there were mony beating hearts
And mony hopes and fears;
And mony were the pray'rs put up
For the young Chevalier.

Oh! Charlie etc.

Lady Nairne

Colin's Cattle

A maiden sang sweetly as a bird on a tree, Crodh Chail-lean, Crodh Chail-lean, Crodh Chail-lean for me; My own Col-in's cat-tle, dap-pled, dun, brown and grey, They return to the milk-ing at the close of the day.

"My own Colin's cattle,
Dappled, dun, brown, and grey,
They return to the milking
At the close of the day.

"In the morning they wander
To their pastures afar,
Where the grass grows the greenest
By corrie and scaur.

"They wander the uplands
Where the soft breezes blow,
And they drink from the fountain
Where the sweet cresses grow.

"But so far as they wander,
Dappled, dun, brown, and grey,
They return to the milking
At the close of the day.

"My bed's in the shian
On the canach's soft down,
But I'd sleep best with Colin
In our sheiling alone."

Thus a maiden sang sweetly
As a bird on a tree,
Cro' Chaillean, Cro' Chaillean,
Cro' Chaillean for me.

***Translated from the Gaelic by
the Rev A Stewart, LLD***

Come O'er the Stream, Charlie

Come o'er the stream, Char-lie, dear Char-lie, brave Char-lie, Come
o'er the stream, Char-lie, and dine wi' Mac-Lean; And though you be
wea-ry we'll make your heart cheer-y, And wel-come our Char-lie, and
his loy-al train. We'll bring down the track dear we'll bring down the
black steer, The lamb from the breck-en and doe from the

glen: The salt sea we'll har-ry, and bring to our Char-lie, The

A   G   D   A

cream from the both-y and curd from the pen.

G   D   G   A   D

And you shall drink freely the dews of Glen Sheerly
That stream in the starlight when kings dinna ken;
And deep be your meed of the wine that is red,
To drink to your sire and his friend the MacLean.

If aught will invite you, or more will delight you,
'Tis ready a troop of our bold Hieland men
Shall range on the heather with bonnet and feather,
Strong arms and broad claymores, three hundred and ten.

Come o'er the stream Charlie, dear Charlie, brave Charlie,
Come o'er the stream, Charlie, and dine wi' MacLean;
And though ye be weary we'll make your heart cheery,
And welcome our Charlie, and his loyal train.

Comin' Thro' the Rye

Gin a bo-dy meet a bo-dy, Com-in' thro' the rye;

Gin a bo-dy kiss a bo-dy, Need a bo - dy cry?

Chorus

Il - ka las-sie has her lad-die, Nane, they say, ha'e I; Yet

a' the lads they smile at me, When com-in' thro' the rye.

Gin a body meet a body
Comin' frae the toon;
Gin a body greet a body,
Need a body froon?

Ilka lassie has her laddie,
Nane, they say, ha'e I;
Yet a' the lads they smile at me,
When comin' thro' the rye.

Amang the train there is a swain
I dearly lo'e mysel';
But what's his name; and what's his hame,
I dinna care to tell.

Ilka lassie has her laddie,
Nane, they say, ha'e I;
Yet a' the lads they smile at me,
When comin' thro' the rye.

Corn Rigs

It was u-pon a—— Lam - mas night, When corn—— rigs are

bon - nie, O, Be - neath the moon's un - cloud - ed light, I held—— a-wa' to——

An - nie,—— O; The time flew by— wi' tent - less heed, Till 'tween the—— late and

ear - ly,—— O, Wi' sma' per-sua - sion she a - greed—— To see me—— thro' the

Chorus

bar - ley,—— O. Corn—— rigs, and bar - ley rigs, Corn—— rigs are

bon - nie___ O; I'll ne'er for - get that hap - py___ night,___ A -
mang the___ rigs wi'___ An - nie,___ O.

D   E   A   D   E
D   E   A

The sky was blue, the wind was still,
The moon was shining clearly, O;
I set her down wi' right good-will
Amang the rigs o' barley, O.
I kent her heart was a' my ain;
I loved her maist sincerely, O;
I kissed her ower and ower again,
Amang the rigs o' barley, O.

Corn rigs, etc.

I locked her in my fond embrace,
Her heart was beating rarely, O;
My blessings on that happy place,
Amang the rigs o' barley, O.
But by the moon and stars so bright,
That shone that hour so clearly, O;
She aye shall bless that happy night
Amang the rigs o' barley, O.

Corn rigs, etc.

I ha'e been blithe wi' comrades dear,
I ha'e been merry drinkin', O;
I ha'e been joyful gatherin' gear;
I ha'e been happy thinkin', O.
But a' the pleasures e'er I saw,
Though three times doubled fairly, O:
That happy night was worth them a',
Amang the rigs o' barley, O.

Corn rigs, etc.   **Robert Burns**

Doun the Burn Davie

When trees did bud and fields were green, And broom bloomed fair to see, When Mary was complete fifteen, And love laughed in her e'e, Blythe Davie's blink her heart did move To speak her mind sae free. Gang doun the burn Davie lad, Doun the burn Davie lad,

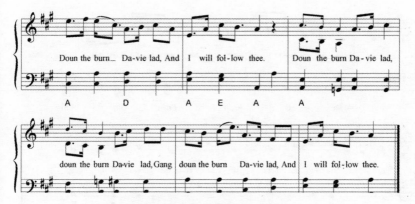

Doun the burn__ Da-vie lad, And I will fol-low thee. Doun the burn Da-vie lad,

A   D   A   E   A   A

doun the burn Da-vie lad, Gang doun the burn   Da-vie lad, And I will fol-low thee.

Now Davie did each lad surpass
That dwelt on yon burnside,
And Mary was the bonniest lass,
Just meet to be a bride.
Thus Davie's blink her heart did move
To speak her mind sae free,
"Gang doun the burn, Davie lad,
Doun the burn, Davie lad,
Doun the burn, Davie lad,
And I will follow thee."

What passed, I guess, was harmless play,
And naething, sure, unmeet,
For ganging hame I heard them say
They liked a walk sae sweet.
Since both were fain their love to own
And speak their mind sae free,
"Gang doun the burn, Davie lad,
Doun the burn, Mary lass,
Doun the burn, my ain dear love,
And aye I'll follow thee."

R Crawford, 1695

Drowned

No won-der my heart it is sore, No won-der the tears that I weep; My

Amin   G   Amin   Emin   Dmin   Emin

true love I'll see him no more, He lies fa-thoms down in the deep.

F   G   Amin   Dmin   Dmin   G   Amin

He lies fathoms down in the deep,
Where the cold clammy seaweeds abound;
How cruel thy wild waves to me,
O sea that my true love hast drowned!

O sea that my true love hast drowned,
Thou hast reft me of joy evermore;
Thy waves make me shudder with fear
As I listen and hear their wild roar.

My true love and I, hand in hand,
Often wandered the uplands among,
Where the wild flowers are freshest to see,
And the wild birds are freest of song;

But alas for the days that are gone,
Alas for my sorrow and me!
Alas that my true love is drowned
Fathoms down in the depths of the sea!

***Translated from the Gaelic by the Rev A
Stewart, LLD***

An Eriskay Love Lilt

Vair me o——— ro van o, Vair me o——— ro van ee, Vair me

o, ru o ho, Sad am I with-out thee. When I'm

Last time only Verse

lone-ly dear white heart, Black the night or wild the sea; By love's

light my foot finds The old path-way to thee.

Vair me o, o rovan o,
Vair me o, o rovan ee,
Vair me o, ru o ho,
Sad am I, without thee.

When I'm lonely, dear white heart,
Black the night or wild the sea;
By love's light my foot finds
The old pathway to thee.

Vair me o, etc.

Thou'rt the music of my heart,
Harp of joy, o cruit mo chridh;
Moon of guidance by night,
Strength and light thou'rt to me.

Vair me o, etc.

Fair Helen of Kirkconnell

I wish I were where Hel - en lies, For night and day on— me she cries; For night and day on— me she cries, I wish I were where Hel - en lies On— fair Kirk-con - nell lea.— Oh Hel - en fair! Oh Hel - en chaste! Were I with thee I— would be blest, Were I with thee I— would be blest, Where thou liest low and at thy rest On— fair Kirk - con - nell— lea.

Oh Helen fair, beyond compare
I'll make a garland of thy hair;
I'll make a garland of thy hair,
Shall bind my heart for evermair
Until the day I dee.
Curst be the heart that hatch'd the thought,
And curst the hand that fired the shot;
And curst the hand that fired the shot,
When in my arms burd Helen dropt,
And died to succour me.

O think na but my heart was sair,
My love dropt down and spak nae mair;
My love dropt down and spak nae mair,
O think na ye my heart was air
On fair Kirkconnell lea.
I found my foe behind a wa';
I lighted doun my sword to draw,
I hacked him in pieces sma,
I hacked him in pieces sma,
Who took my love from me.

I wish I were where Helen lies,
For night and day on me she cries;
I wish I were where Helen lies
On fair Kirkconnell lea.

Fair Young Mary

Mhai-ri bhan og, my ain on-ly dea-rie, My win-some my bon-nie wee bride,

Em   G   Emin   Amin   D   G

Let the world gang and a' the lave wi' it, Gin ye are but left by my side.____ The

Emin   C   G   Amin   B7   Emin

lark to its nest, the stream to the o-cean, The star to its home in the west___ And

Emin   D   D7   G   Emin   Amin   D   G

I to my Ma-ry and I to my dar-ling, And I to the ane I lo'e best.

C   G   D7   G   Emin   Amin   B7   Emin

Time sall na touch thee, nor trouble come near
  thee,
Thou maunna grow old like the lave,
And gin ye gang, Mary, the way o' the weary,
I'll follow thee soon to the grave.
A glance o' thy e'en wad banish a' sorrow,
A smile, and fareweel to a' strife,
For peace is beside thee, and joy is around thee,
And love is the light o' thy life.

A C MacLeod

Farewell to Fiunary

The wind is fair, the day is fine, And swift-ly, swift-ly runs the time; The

G   C   D   Emin   C   D

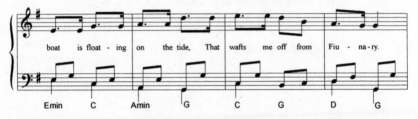

boat is float-ing on the tide, That wafts me off from Fiu-na-ry.

Emin   C   Amin   G   C   G   D   G

Chorus

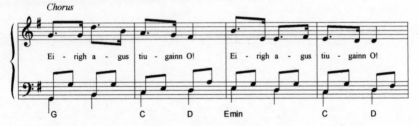

Ei - righ a - gus tiu - gainn O!   Ei - righ a - gus tiu - gainn O!

G   C   D   Emin   C   D

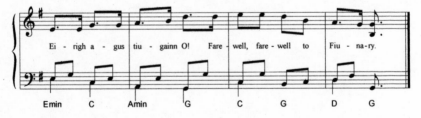

Ei - righ a - gus tiu - gainn O! Fare-well, fare-well to Fiu-na-ry.

Emin   C   Amin   G   C   G   D   G

A thousand, thousand tender ties
Awake this day my plaintive sighs;
My heart within me almost dies,
At thought of leaving Fiunary.

We must up and haste away,
We must up and haste away,
We must up and haste away,
Farewell, farewell to Fiunary.

But I must leave these happy vales,
See, they spread the flapping sails!
Adieu, adieu my native dales,
Farewell, farewell, to Fiunary.

We must up etc.

Norman MacLeod

The Flowers o' the Forest

I've seen the smi - ling of For - tune be- guil - ing, I've

tast - ed her fa - vours and felt her de- cay:

Sweet was her bless - ing and kind her ca - ress - ing, But

now they are fled, fled far a- way.

I've seen the for - est a - dorn'd the fore - most Wi'

flowers o' the fair - est baith pleas - ant and gay, Sae
bon - nie was their bloom - ing, their scent the air per - fu - ming, But
now they are with - er'd and a' wede a - way.

I've seen the morning wi' gold the hills adorning,
And loud tempests roaring before parting day;
I've seen Tweed's silver streams, glitt'ring in the sunny beams,
Grow drumlie and dark as they roll'd on their way.

O fickle fortune, why this cruel sporting?
Why so perplex us poor sons of a day?
The frown cannot fear me; thy smile cannot cheer me,
Since the Flowers o' the Forest are a' wede away.

The Flower of Scotland

O flower of Scot - - land, When will we see Your like a - gain,

That fought and died for Your wee bit hill and glen, And stood a -

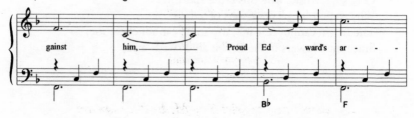

gainst him, Proud Ed - ward's ar - - -

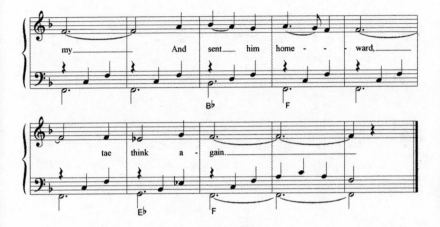

The hills are bare now,
And autumn leaves lie thick and still,
O'er land that is lost now,
Which those so dearly held,
That stood against him,
Proud Edward's army,
And sent him homeward,
Tae think again.

Those days are past now,
And in the past they must remain,
But we can still rise now,
And be the nation again,
That stood against him,
Proud Edward's army,
And sent him homeward,
Tae think again.

Words and music: Roy M. B. Williamson
© The Corries (Music) Ltd.

Flow Gently, Sweet Afton

Flow gent - ly, sweet Af - ton a - mang thy green braes,— Flow gent - ly, I'll— sing thee a— song in— thy— praise; My— Ma - ry's a - sleep by thy mur - mur - ing stream, Flow gent- ly, sweet Af - ton, dis - turb not— her— dream.

E · F#min · E · F#
Bsus4 B · E · F#min B7 C#min · E · B7
E · E7 · C#min · A · E · F#min
Bsus4 B · E · B E A · E/B B7 · E

Thou stockdove whose echo resounds thro' the glen,
Ye wild whistling blackbirds in yon thorny den;
Thou green-crested lapwing, thy screaming forbear –
I charge you, disturb not my slumbering fair.

How pleasant thy banks, thy green valleys below,
Where wild in the woodlands the primroses blow;
There oft as mild ev'ning sweeps over the lea,
The sweet-scented birk shades my Mary and me.

Thy crystal stream, Afton, how lovely it glides
And winds by the cot where my Mary resides;
How wanton thy waters her snowy feet lave,
As gath'ring sweet flow'rets she stems thy clear wave.

Flow gently, sweet Afton, among thy green braes,
Flow gently, sweet river, the theme of my lays;
My Mary's asleep by thy murmuring stream,
Flow gently, sweet Afton, disturb not her dream.

Robert Burns

The Four Maries

Yes - treen the Queen had four Ma - ries, The nicht she'll ha'e but

three; There was Ma - rie Sea - ton, And Ma - rie Bea - ton, And

Ma - rie Car - mi - chael and me. Oh oft - en ha'e I dress'd my Queen, And

deck'd wi' gowd her hair, And she has gien me

in re - turn A hem - pen scarf to wear.

I ha'e but just begun to live,
And yet this day I dee;
Oh, tie a napkin ower my face,
That the gallows I mayna see.

My father kissed me and little thought,
When last he looked on me,
That I his last and lo'eliest wean
Should hang on a gallows tree.

Oh little did my mother ken,
The day she gi'ed me breath,
That I should come sae far frae hame
And die a shameful death.

For if my father and mother got wit,
And my bold brethren three,
Oh, mickle wad be the guid red blood
That day wad be spilt for me.

Glenlogie

"O haud your tongue, dochter, ye'll get better than he."
"O say na sae, mither, for that canna be.
Though Drumlie is richer and greater than he,
Yet if I maun wed him I'll certainly dee."

"Where will I get a bonnie boy to win hose and shoon,
Will gae to Glenlogie and come again soon?"
"O here am I, a bonnie boy, to win hose and shoon,
Will gae to Glenlogie and come again soon."

When he gaed to Glenlogie 'twas "Wash and go dine,"
'Twas "Wash ye my pretty boy, wash and go dine."
"O 'twas ne'er my father's fashion and it ne'er shall be mine
To gar a lady's errand wait till I dine;

"But there is, Glenlogie, a letter for thee."
The first line he read a low smile gi'ed he,
The neist line he read the tear blindit his e'e,
But the last line he read he gart the table flee.

"Gae saddle the black horse, gae saddle the brown,
Gae saddle the swiftest steed e'er rade frae toun."
But lang ere the horse was brocht round to the green,
O bonnie Glenlogie was twa mile his lane.

When he cam' to Glenfeldy's door sma' mirth was there,
Bonnie Jean's mither was rivin' her hair.
"Ye're welcome, Glenlogie, ye're welcome," said she,
"Ye're welcome, Glenlogie, your Jeanie to see."

Pale and wan was she when Glenlogie gaed ben,
But red rosy grew she whene'er he sat doun;
She turned awa' her head, but the smile was in her e'e,
"O binna feared, mither, I'll maybe no dee."

Old Scottish Ballad

Green Grow the Rashes, O!

There's nought but care on ev-'ry han', In ev-'ry hour that pass-es, O; What

sig - ni-fies the life o' man, An' 'twere na for the lass-es, O.

Chorus
Green grow the rash-es, O! Green grow the rash-es, O! The

sweet-est hours that e'er I spend, Are spent a-mang the lass-es, O!

The warldly race may riches chase,
An' riches still may fly them, O;
And though at last they catch them fast,
Their hearts can ne'er enjoy them, O.

Green grow the rashes, O!
Green grow the rashes, O!
The sweetest hours that e'er I spend,
Are spent amang the lasses, O!

Gi'e me a canny hour at e'en,
My arms about my dearie, O;
An' warldly cares, and warldly men
May a' gae tapsalteerie, O.

Green grow etc.

For you sae douce, wha sneer at this,
Ye're nought but senseless asses, O;
The wisest man the warld e'er saw,
He dearly loved the lasses, O.

Green grow etc.

Auld Nature swears, the lovely dears
Her noblest work she classes, O;
Her prentice han' she tried on man,
And then she made the lasses, O.

Green grow etc.

Robert Burns

Health and Joy Be With You

Health and joy be with you, My bon - nie nut - brown maid, With
tres - ses rich - ly flow - ing, With vir - gin grace ar - rayed; Thy
voice to me is mu - sic, When hea - vy I may be; It

heals my heart's deep sor - row To speak a word with thee.

In sadness I am rocking
This night upon the sea,
For troubled is my slumber
When thy smile is far from me;
On thee I'm ever thinking,
Thy face is ever near,
And if I may not find thee
Then death alone is dear.

Before we heaved our anchor
Their evil speech began,
That you no more should see me,
The false and faithless man.
Droop not thy head, my darling,
My heart is all thine own,
No power on earth can part us,
But cruel death alone.

**Translated from the Gaelic by
Professor Blackie**

A Hieland Lad

A— Hie-land lad my— love was born, The Law-land laws he—

held in scorn; But he still was faith—fu'— to his clan, My— gal-lant braw— John—

Chorus

Hie-land man. Sing— hey! my braw John Hie-land man! Sing

ho! my braw John— Hie-land man! There's no' a lad— in—

a' the lan' Was— match— for— my— John Hie-land-man!

Wi' his philabeg and his tartan plaid,
And gude claymore down by his side;
The ladies' hearts he did trepan –
My gallant braw John Hielandman!

Sing hey! my braw John Hielandman,
Sing ho! my braw John Hielandman,
There's no a lad in a' the lan'
Was match for my John Hielandman.

They banish'd him beyond the sea,
But ere the bud was on the tree,
Adown my cheek the pearlies ran,
Embracing my John Hielandman.

Sing hey! etc.

But oh, they caught him at the last,
And bound him in a dungeon fast;
My curse upon them every wan –
They've hanged my braw John Hielandman!

Sing hey! etc.

Robert Burns (extract from the Jolly Beggars)

Ho-ro, My Nut-Brown Maiden

Ho-ro my nut-brown maid-en, Hi-ri my nut-brown maid-en, Ho-

F   Bb   F   C7   F   Bb   C

ro - ro,   maid - en! Oh she's the maid for me.

F   Amin Dmin   F   C7   F

Her eye so mild-ly beam-ing, Her look so frank and free, In

F   C

wak-ing and in dream-ing, Is ev-er-more with me.

F   Bb   F/C   C7   F

O Mary, mild-eyed Mary,
By land, or on the sea,
Though time and tide may vary,
My heart beats true to thee.

Ho-ro my nut-brown maiden,
Hi-ri my nut brown maiden,
Ho-ro-ro, maiden!
Oh, she's the maid for me.

In Glasgow or Dunedin
Were maidens fair to see;
But ne'er a Lowland maiden
Could lure mine eyes from thee;

Ho-ro, etc.

Mine eyes that never vary
From looking to the glen,
Where dwells my Highland Mary
Like wild-rose 'neath the Ben.

Ho-ro, etc.

And when with blossom laden,
Bright summer comes again,
I'll fetch my nut-brown maiden
Down frae the bonnie glen.

Ho-ro, etc.

How Can Ye Gang, Lassie?

O how can ye gang las-sie, How can ye gang? O
how can ye gang sae to grieve me? Wi' your beau-ty and your art Ye hae
bro-ken my heart,__ For I nev-er, nev-er thocht ye wad leave me.

"O, how could ye think, Jamie,
How could ye think,
O, how could ye think that I lo'ed ye?
For its O and I lo'e ane,
But I daurna tell his name,
And I never, never meant to deceive ye."

"Then how could ye look, Jeannie,
How could ye look?
And what when your e'en met mine, lass?
For wi' sorrow in my heart,
And the tears in my e'en,
I maun down to the grave loving thee, lass."

Old Scottish Song

I Lo'e Na a Laddie but Ane

I lo'e na a lad-die but ane,___ He lo'es na a las - sie but me;___ He's wil - lin' to make me his ain,___ And his ain I am wil - lin' to be.___ He coft me a rok - ley o' blue___ And a pair___ o' mit - tens sae green;___ He vow'd that he'd ev - er be true,___ And I plight - ed my troth___ yes - treen.___

Let ithers brag weel o' their gear,
Their land and their lordly degree,
I care na for aught but my dear,
For he's ilka thing lordly to me.
His words mair than sugar are sweet,
His sense drives ilk fear far awa';
I listen, poor fool, and I greet –
But how sweet are the tears as they fa'!

"Dear lassie," he cries wi' a jeer,
"Ne'er heed what the auld anes will say;
Though we've little to brag of, ne'er fear,
What's gowd to a heart that is wae?
Our laird has both honours and wealth,
Yet see how he's dwinin' wi' care;
Now we, though we've naething but health,
Are canty and leal ever mair."

"O Menie, the heart that is true
Has something mair precious than gear;
Ilk night it has naething to rue;
Ilk morn it has naething to fear.
Ye warldlings gae hoard up your store,
And tremble for fear lest ye tine;
Guard your treasure wi' lock, bar and door –
True love is the guardian o' mine."

A Jacobite Lament

It was all___ for our right - ful king That we left fair Scot - land's strand;___ It was

Amin G F G Amin G F

all___ for our right - ful king That we e'er saw I - rish___ land, my_ dear, We

G F C Dmin C G C

e'er___ saw I - rish land, my dear, We e'er___ saw I - rish land.___

Amin G F Amin Emin Amin

Now a' is done that men can do,
And a' is done in vain;
My love an' native land, fareweel,
For I maun cross the main, my dear,
For I maun cross the main.

He turned him right an' round about,
All on the Irish shore,
He ga'e his bridle-reins a shake,
Wi' "Adieu for evermore, my dear,
Adieu for evermore."

The sodger frae the wars returns,
The sailor frae the main;
But I ha'e parted frae my love,
Never to meet again, my dear,
Never to meet again.

When day is gane, an' night is come,
An' a' folk boun' to sleep,
I think on him that's far awa',
The lee-lang night, an' weep, my dear,
The lee-lang night, an' weep.

Attributed to Captain Ogilvy, 1690

Jock o' Hazeldean

"Why weep ye by the tide, la - dye, Why weep ye by the tide?___ I'll wed ye to my young - est son, And ye shall be his bride; And ye shall be his bride, la - dye, Sae come - ly to___ be seen:" But aye she loot the tears down fa, For Jock o' Ha - zel - dean.

"Now let this wilful grief be done,
And dry that cheek so pale:
Young Frank is chief of Errington,
And lord of Langley-dale.
His step is first in peacefu' ha',
His sword in battle keen."
But aye she loot the tear doon fa'
For Jock o' Hazeldean.

"A chain of gowd ye shall not lack,
Nor braid to bind your hair;
Nor mettled hound, nor managed hawk,
Nor palfrey fresh and fair.
And you the foremost o' them a'
Shall ride our forest queen."
But aye she loot the tear doon fa'
Foe Jock o' Hazeldean.

The kirk was deck'd at morning-tide,
The tapers glimmer'd fair;
The priest and bridegroom wait the bride,
But ne'er a bride was there.
They sought her baith by bower and ha':
The ladye wasna seen;
She's ower the Border and awa'
Wi' Jock o' Hazeldean.

Joy of My Heart

Red, red, is the path to glo - ry, Thick yon ban - ners

Emin   Amin   D   Amin   G

meet the sky, O my Geor - die, death's be - fore ye,

D   Emin Bmin   D   G   Amin   D

Turn and hear my bo - ding cry. Joy of my heart,

Amin   Emin   Amin   B   Emin   C   G

Geor - die a - gain, Joy of my heart, Stu mo run.

D   C   G   Amin Bmin7 Emin

Turn and see thy tartan plaidie
Rising o'er my broken heart,
O my bonnie Highland laddie
Sad am I with thee to part.
Joy of my heart, Geordie agam,
Joy of my heart, 'stu mo run.

Dr Robert Couper, of Fochabers, 1799

Lament for Maclean of Ardgour

Wail___ loud - ly ye wo - men your co - ro - nach dole - ful, La -

C   E   Amin

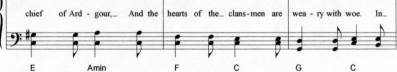

ment him ye pi - pers, tread so - lemn and slow; Mown_ down like a flower is the

F   C   C   G   C

chief of Ard - gour,__ And the hearts of the_ clans - men are wea - ry with woe. In_

E   Amin   F   C   G   C

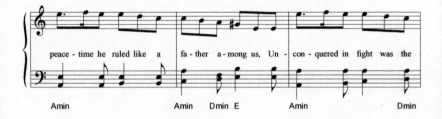

peace - time he ruled like a fa - ther a - mong us, Un - con - quered in fight was the

Amin   Amin   Dmin E   Amin   Dmin

blade that he bore; But the chase was the glo-ry and
C F G C

pride of his man-hood, Strong Don-ald the hun-ter, Mac - gil - li-an More.
E Amin F C G C

Low down by yon burn that's half hidden with heather
He lurked like a lion in the lair he knew well;
'Twas there sobbed the red-deer to feel his keen dagger,
There pierced by his arrow the cailzie-cock fell.
How oft when at e'en he would watch for the wild fowl,
Like lightning his coracle sped from the shore;
But still, and for aye, as we cross the lone lochan,
Is Donald the hunter, Macgillian More!

Once more let his war-cry resound in the mountains,
Macdonalds shall hear it in eerie Glencoe,
Its echoes shall float o'er the braes of Lochaber,
Till Stewarts at Appin that slogan shall know;
And borne to the waters beyond the Loch Linnhe,
'Twixt Morven and Mull where the tide-eddies roar,
Macgillians shall hear it and mourn for their kinsman,
For Donald the hunter, Macgillian More.

Then here let him rest in the lap of Scaur Donald,
The wind for his watcher, the mist for his shroud,
Where the green and the grey moss will weave their wild
    tartans,
A covering meet for a chieftain so proud.
For, free as the eagle, these rocks were his eyrie,
And free as the eagle his spirit shall soar
O'er the crags and the corries that erst knew the footfall
Of Donald the hunter, Macgillian More.

Harold Boulton

Leezie Lindsay

Will ye gang to the Hie-lands, Lee-zie Lind-say? Will ye

D   A   D

gang to the Hie-lands wi' me? Will ye

D   A   Bm

gang to the Hie-lands, Lee-zie Lind-say, My

D   A   D

bride and my dar-ling to be?

G   D   A   D

"To gang to the Hielands wi' you, sir?
I dinna ken how that may be,
For I ken na the land that ye live in,
Nor ken I the lad I'm gaun' wi'."

"Leezie, lassie, 'tis little that ye ken,
If sae be ye dinna ken me,
For my name is Lord Ronald Macdonald,
A chieftain o' high degree."

She has kilted her coats o' green satin,
She has kilted them up to the knee,
And she's aff wi' Lord Ronald Macdonald
His bride and his darling to be.

Old Scottish Ballad

A Lewis Bridal Song

I'd sail with you to Mia-vaig in Uig, E'en tho' in twi-light, e'en tho' in twi-light.

I'd sail with you to Mia-vaig in Uig, E'en thro' the dark and the sea - mist.

How shall we fare when the wind's in the sail, and storm clouds ga - ther,

storm clouds ga - ther? How shall we fare in the whirl of the gale

Out in the midst of the Is - lands? Mo - rag bheag of the gold - en hair,
Who is the maid - en who dances with joy, Like

Fair as the dawn - ing, fair as the dawn - ing, Mo - rag bheag of the
foam on the wave - tops, foam on the wave - tops? Who is the maid on the

Bmin   B7   Emin   C   G

gold - en hair, Light - ly she stepped to her bri - dal.
danc - ing floor? She is the bride who came sail - ing.

C   G   Bmin   D   C

Linten Lowrin

I sheared my first hairst in Bog - end, Doun by the fit o' Ben - a - chie; And

sair I wrought and sair I fought But I wan out my pen - ny fee;

Lin - ten low - rin, low - rin lin - ten, Lin - ten low - rin lin - ten lee: I'll

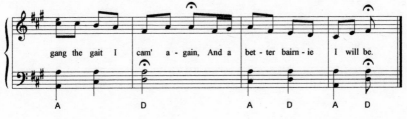

gang the gait I cam' a - gain, And a bet - ter bairn - ie I will be.

O! Rhynie's wark is ill to work,
And Rhynie's wages are but sma';
And Rhynie's laws are double straight,
And that does grieve me maist of a'.

Linten lowrin, lowrin linten,
Linten lowrin, linten lee;
I'll gang the gait I cam' again,
And a better bairnie I will be.

O! Rhynie is a Hieland place,
It doesna suit a Lawland loon;
And Rhynie is a cauld clay hole,
It is na like my faither's toun.

Linten lowrin, etc.

Old Aberdeenshire Song

Loch Lomond

By yon bon - nie banks and by yon bon - nie braes, Where the
sun shines bright on Loch Lo - mond, Where me and my true love were
e - ver wont to gae, On the bon - nie, bon - nie banks o' Loch Lo - mond. O,
ye'll tak' the high road, an' I'll tak' the low road, An' I'll be in Scot - land a -
fore ye; But me and my true love will ne - ver meet a - gain On the

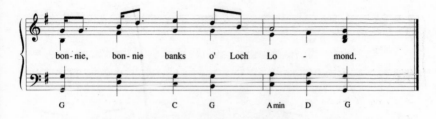

bon - nie,   bon - nie   banks   o'   Loch   Lo   -   mond.

G   C   G   A min   D   G

'Twas there that we parted in yon shady glen,
On the steep, steep side o' Ben Lomond
Where in purple hue, the Hieland hills we viewed;
And the moon comin' out in the gloamin'.

O, ye'll tak' the high road, an' I'll tak' the low road,
An' I'll be in Scotland afore ye;
But me and my true love will never meet again
On the bonnie, bonnie banks o' Loch Lomond.

The wee birdies sing, and the wild flowers spring,
While in sunshine the waters are sleeping;
But the broken heart kens nae second spring again,
Though the waefu' may cease frae their greetin'.

O, ye'll tak' the high road, etc.

Lady John Douglas Scott

A Lyke Wake Dirge

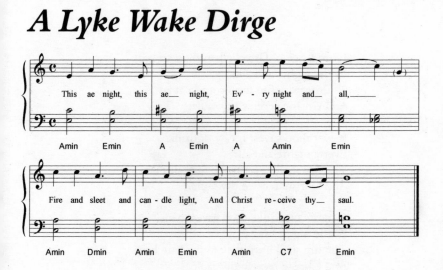

This ae night, this ae night, Ev'-ry night and all,

Amin   Emin   A   Emin   A   Amin   Emin

Fire and sleet and can-dle light, And Christ re-ceive thy saul.

Amin   Dmin   Amin   Emin   Amin   C7   Emin

When from hence away thou'rt past,
Everie nighte and alle,
To Whinny-muir thou comest at last,
And Christe receive thy saule.

If ever thou gavest hosen and shoon,
Everie nighte and alle,
Sit thee doun and put them on,
And Christe receive thy saule.

If hosen and shoon thou gavest nane,
Everie nighte and alle,
The whinnes shall pricke thee to the bare bane,
And Christe receive thy saule.

From Whinny-muir when thou art past,
Everie nighte and alle,
To Brigg o' Dread thou comest at last,
And Christe receive thy saule.

From Brigg o' Dread when thou art past,
Everie nighte and alle,
To Purgatory fire thou comest at last,
And Christe receive thy saule.

If ever thou gavest meate or drinke,
Everie nighte and alle,
The fire shall never make thee shrinke,
And Christe receive thy saule.

If meate or drinke thou gavest nane,
Everie nighte and alle,
The fire shall burn thee to the bare bane,
And Christe receive thy saule.

This ae nighte, this ae nighte,
Everie nighte and alle,
Fire and sleete and candle-lighte,
And Christe receive thy saule.

**A chant sung by those keeping
watch over a corpse**

Macpherson's Rant

Fare - weel ye dun - geons dark and strong, Fare - weel, fare - weel to

thee. Mac - pher - son's time will no be_ long On

Chorus

yon - der gal - lows tree. Sae ran - tin' - ly, sae wan - ton - ly, Sae

daun - tin' - ly gaed he, He played a tune and he

(Last time)

daunced it roun' A - bou' the gal - lows tree.

'Twas by a woman's treacherous hand
That I was condemn'd to dee.
Above my head at a window she stood
And a blanket threw ower me.

Sae rantin'ly, sae wantonly,
Sae dauntin'ly gaed he,
He played a tune, and he danced it roun'
About the gallows tree.

Untie these bands fae aff my hands
And gi'e tae me my sword;
And there's nae a man in all Scotlan',
But I'll brave him at a word.

Sae rantin'ly etc.

There's some come here for tae see me hang,
And some tae buy my fiddle;
But ere I come tae pairt wi' her,
I'll brak her doon the middle.

Sae rantin'ly etc.

He took his fiddle in baith his hands
And brak it ower his knee;
And said, when I am deid and gone
Nae ither shall play thee.

Sae rantin'ly, etc.

The courier came ower the brig o' Banff
Tae set Macpherson free –
But they put the clock a quarter afore,
And hanged him fae the tree.

Sae rantin'ly, sae wantonly,
Sae dauntin'ly gaed he,
He played a tune, and he danced it roun'
About the gallows tree.

Mary of Argyle

I have heard the ma- vis sing- ing His love song to the morn; I have
G   C   G   Amin   D   G

seen the dew- drop cling- ing To the rose just new - ly born; But a
C   G   D7   G

sweet - er song has cheer'd me, At the ev' - ning's gen - tle close; And I've
Emin   B7   Bmin   Emin

seen an eye still bright- er Than the dew- drop on the rose. 'Twas thy
A7   D   A7   D

voice my gen- tle Ma- ry, And thine art - less win - ning smile, That
G   C   G   Amin   D   G

made this world an E - den Bon - ny Ma - ry of__ Ar - gyle.

Tho' thy voice may lose its sweetness,
And thine eye its brightness too;
Tho' thy step may lack its fleetness,
And thy hair its sunny hue;
Still to me wilt thou be dearer
Than all the world shall own –
I have loved thee for thy beauty,
But not for that alone.
I have watch'd thy heart, dear Mary,
And its goodness was the wile
That has made thee mine for ever,
Bonny Mary of Argyle.

My Ain Kind Dearie

When o'er the hill the east-ern star Tells bught in' time is near, my jo, And
ow - sen frae the fur - row'd field Re - turn sae dowf and wear - ie O; Down
by the burn, where scent - ed birks Wi' dew are hang - ing clear, my jo, I'll
meet thee on the lea - rig; My ain kind dear - ie, O.

In mirkest glen at midnight hour
I'd rove and ne'er be eerie, O,
If thro' that glen I gae'd to thee,
My ain kind dearie, O.
Altho' the nicht were ne'er sae wild,
And I were ne'er sae weary, O,
I'd meet thee on the lea-rig,
My ain kind dearie, O.

The hunter lo'es the morning sun,
To rouse the mountain deer, my jo;
At noon the fisher seeks the glen,
Along the burn to steer, my jo;
Gi'e me the hour o' gloamin' grey,
It maks my heart sae cheerie, O,
To meet thee on the lea-rig,
My ain kind dearie, O.

Robert Burns

My Dark-haired Maid

Mo nigh-ean dhu, the hills are bright, And on this last and love-ly night, I'd

C   Emin   C   F   C   Emin   G7   C   F

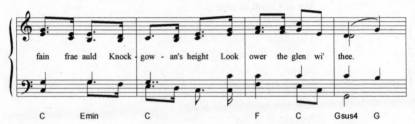

fain frae auld Knock-gow-an's height Look ower the glen wi' thee.

C   Emin   C   F   C   Gsus4   G

Ne-ver mair we'll tread its hea-ther, Ne-ver doun the lea

C   G   C7   Dmin   C   F   C   E   Amin

Lil-tin' will we shear the-gi-ther, Fu' o' mirth and glee. - -

C   Dmin   Emin   E7   Amin   F   C   Gsus4   G

For - tune's blasts o' win - try wea - ther Drive us ower the sea, But

C   G C7 Dmin C F   C   E   Amin   A

lang's we're blest wi' ane a - ni - ther Fie! let fears gae flee.____ Yet

Dmin   A   Dmin   G   F   C   Gsus4   G

see, my dear, the hills are bright, And on this last and love - ly night, I'd

C   Emin   C   F   C   Emin   G7   C F

fain frae auld Knock - gow - an's height Look ower the glen wi' thee.____

C   E   Dmin   C   Amin   D9 G   C

Mo nighean dhu, 'twas there we met,
And O! that hour is precious yet,
When first my honest vow could get
Love's tearfu' smile frae thee.
Hearts were pledg'd ere either knew it,
What's to be maun be,
Mine was tint ere I could trow o't
Wi' that glancing e'e.
Dear Knockgowan and the view o't
Ne'er again we'll see,
Let me gang and tak' adieu o't
Laoth ma chree, wi' thee.
Mo nighean dhu, 'twas there we met,
And O! that hour is precious yet,
When first my honest vow could get
Love's tearfu' smile frae thee.

Dr John Park

My Faithful Fond One

If wings were mine now to skim the brine now,
And like a sea-gull to float me free,
To Islay's shore now they'd bear me o'er now,
Where dwells the maiden that's dear to me.

My fair and rare one, my faithful fond one,
My faithful fair, wilt not come to me.
On a bed of pain here who remain here
With weary longing for the sight of thee?

O were I yonder with her to wander
Beneath the green hills beside the sea,
With birds in chorus that warble o'er us,
And ruth of kisses so sweet to me!

My fair and rare one, my faithful fond one,
My faithful fair, wilt not come to me.
On a bed of pain here who remain here
With weary longing for the sight of thee?

What though the sky here be wet or dry here,
With peaceful breeze here, or windy war,
In winter glooming or summer blooming
'Tis all one season, love, when thou art far.

My fair and rare one, my faithful fond one,
My faithful fair, wilt not come to me.
On a bed of pain here who remain here
With weary longing for the sight of thee?

My Love's in Germanie

My love's in Ger - ma - nie, Send him hame, send him hame, My love's in Ger - ma - nie, send him hame. My love's in Ger - ma - nie, Fight - ing brave for roy - al - ty; He may ne'er his Jean - nie see, Send him hame, send him hame, He may ne'er his Jean - nie see, Send him hame.

He's brave as brave can be,
Send him hame, send him hame;
He's brave as brave can be, send him hame!
He's brave as brave can be,
He wad rather fa' than flee,
But his life is dear to me,
Send him hame, send him hame;
But his life is dear to me, send him hame!

His faes are ten to three,
Send him hame, send him hame;
His faes are ten to three, send him hame!
His faes are ten to three,
He maun either fa' or flee;
In the cause o' loyalty
Send him hame, send him hame;
In the cause o' loyalty send him hame!

Your love ne'er learnt to flee,
Bonnie dame, winsome dame;
Your love ne'er learnt to flee, winsome dame!
Your love ne'er learnt to flee,
But he fell in Germanie
Fighting brave for royalty,
Bonnie dame, mournfu' dame;
Fighting brave for royalty, mournfu' dame!

He'll ne'er come owre the sea,
Willie's slain, Willie's slain;
He'll ne'er come owre the sea, Willie's gane!
He'll ne'er come owre the sea
To his love and ain countree;
This warld's nae mair for me,
Willie's gane, Willie's gane;
This warld's nae mair for me, Willie's slain.

Hector MacNeil

My Love Is Like a Red, Red Rose

Oh my love is like a red, red rose, That's new - ly sprung in June; Oh my— love is like the mel - o - dy That's sweet - ly played in tune. As fair thou art, my bon - nie lass, So deep in love am I; And— I will love thee still, my dear, Till a' the seas gang dry; Till— a' the seas gang dry, my dear, Till a' the seas gang dry; And—

Till a' the seas gang dry, my dear,
And the rocks melt wi' the sun;
And I will love thee still, my dear,
While the sands o' life shall run.

While the sands o' life shall run, my dear,
While the sands o' life shall run;
And I will love thee still, my dear,
While the sands o' life shall run.

And fare thee weel, my only love,
O fare thee weel a while;
And I will come again, my love,
Tho' 'twere ten thousand mile.

Tho' 'twere ten thousand mile, my love,
Tho' 'twere ten thousand mile;
And I will come again, my love,
Tho' 'twere ten thousand mile.

Robert Burns

My Love, She's But a Lassie Yet

My love she's but a lass - ie yet, My love she's but a lass - ie yet, We'll let her stand a year or twa, She'll no be half sae sau - cy yet. I rue the day I socht her, O I rue the day I socht her, O Wha gets her need - na say she's woo'd, But he may say he's bocht her, O!

Come draw a drap o' the best o't yet,
Come draw a drap o' the best o't yet;
Gae seek for pleasure where ye will,
But here I never missed it yet,

We're a' a dry wi' drinkin' o't,
We're a' a dry wi' drinkin' o't;
The minister kissed the fiddler's wife
And couldna preach for thinkin' o't.

Robert Burns

O Can Ye Sew Cushions?

O can ye sew cu-shions, and can ye sew sheets, And can ye sing bal-la-loo when the bair-nie greets? And hie and baw bir-die and hie and baw lamb, And hie and baw bir-die, my bon-nie wee lamb.

Heigh O! Heugh O! what'll I do wi' ye? Black's the life that I lead wi' ye; Mo-ny o' ye, lit-tle to gie ye, Heigh O! Heugh O! what'll I do wi' ye?

Now hush-a-baw lammie,
And hush-a-baw dear,
Now hush-a-baw lammie,
Thy minnie is here.
The wild wind is ravin',
Thy minnie's heart's sair,
The wild wind is ravin'
And ye dinna care.

Heigh O, heugh O, what'll I do wi' ye?
Black's the life that I lead wi' ye;
Mony o' ye, little to gie ye,
Heigh O, heugh O, what'll I do wi' ye.

Sing ballaloo lammie,
Sing ballaloo dear,
Does wee lammie ken
That its daddie's no here?
Ye're rockin' fu' sweetly
On mammie's warm knee,
But daddie's a rockin'
Upon the saut sea.

Heigh O, heugh O, etc.

Old Scottish Song

O Gin I Were Where Gowdie Rins

Oh— gin I— were where— Gow-die rins, where— Gow-die rins, where—

A D A D A C#

Fine

Gow-die rins;— O— gin I— were where— Gow-die rins at the back o' Ben-a— chie.

D E A D A E A

Ance mair to hear the wild bird's sang, To wan-der birks and braes— a-mang, 'Midst

A D A A D

D.C.

friends and fav'-rites left sae lang, At the back o' Ben-a-chie.

A D A D A

130

O mony a day in blithe spring-time,
O mony a day in summer's prime,
I've wand'ring wiled awa' the time
At the back o' Benachie.

O gin I were, where Gowdie rins,
Where Gowdie rins, where Gowdie rins,
O gin I were where Gowdie rins
At the back o' Benachie!

O there wi' Jean on ilka night,
When baith our hearts were young and light,
We've wandered by the cool moonlight
At the back o' Benachie.

O gin I were, &c., &c., &c.

O fortune's flow'rs wi' thorns are rife,
And wealth is won wi' toil and strife;
Ae day gie me o' youthful life
At the back o' Benachie!

O gin I were, &c., &c., &c.

Dr John Park

O May, Thy Morn Was Ne'er Sae Sweet

O May, thy morn was ne'er sae sweet as the mirk night o' De-
cem - ber! For spark - ling was the ro - sy wine, And pri - vate was the
cham - ber: And dear was she I dare - na name, But
I will ay re - mem - ber: And dear was she I
dare - na name: But I will ay re - mem - ber.

And here's tae them that, like oursel
Can push about the jorum;
And here's tae them that wish us weel –
May a' that's guid watch o'er them.
And here's tae them we daurna tell –
The dearest o' the quorum!

Robert Burns

O'er the Moor

O'er the moor I wan - der lone - ly, Och - on - a - rie, my

G   Emin   G   D   G   Emin

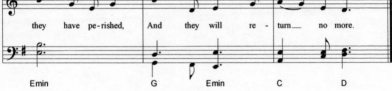

heart__ is sore; Where are all the joys I che__ rished? With my dar - ling

Amin   D   Bmin   G   Bmin   C   G   D

they have pe - rished, And they will re - turn__ no more.

Emin   G   Emin   C   D

I loved thee first, I loved thee only,
Ochon-a-rie, my heart is sore;
I loved thee from the day I met thee,
What care I though all forget thee?
I will love thee evermore.

A C MacLeod

The Piper o' Dundee

The pi - per came tae oor toon, tae oor— toon, tae oor— toon, The

pi - per came tae oor toon, And he played bon - ni - lie. He

play'd a spring, the Laird to please, A spring brent new frae yont the seas; And

then he gae'd his bags a heeze, And play'd an - i - ther key. And was - na he a ro - guie, a

ro - guie, a ro - guie, And was - na he a ro - guie, The pi - per o' Dun - dee?

He play'd "The Welcome owre the Main",
And "Ye'se be Fou' and I'se be Fain",
And "Auld Stuart's Back Again",
Wi' muckle mirth and glee.
He play'd "The Kirk", he play'd "The Quier",
The "Mullin Dhu" and "Chevalier",
And "Lang Awa', but Welcome Here",
Sae sweet, sae bonnilie.

And wasna he a roguie, a roguie, a roguie?
And wasna he a roguie,
The piper o' Dundee?

It's some gat swords, and some gat nane,
And some were dancing mad their lane;
And mony a vow o' weir was ta'en
That night at Amulree.
There was Tullibardine, and Burleigh,
And Struan, Keith and Ogilvie;
And brave Carnegie, wha but he,
The piper o' Dundee!

And wasna he etc.

The Praise of Islay

Though its shore is rocky, drear,
Early doth the sun appear
On leafy brake and fallow deer,
And flocks and herds in Islay.

O my dear, my native isle,
Nought from thee my heart can wile,
O my dear, my native isle,
My heart beats true to Islay.

Eagles rise on soaring wing,
Herons watch the gushing spring,
Heath-cocks with their whirring bring
Their own delight to Islay.

O my dear, etc.

Birken branches there are gay,
Hawthorns wave their silvered spray,
Every bough the breezes sway
Awakens joy in Islay.

O my dear, etc.

Mavis sings on hazel bough,
Linnets haunt the glen below,
O may long their wild notes flow
With melodies in Islay.

O my dear, etc.

Translated from the Gaelic by
Thomas Pattison

Proud Maisie

Proud Mai - sie is in the wood, Walk - ing so ear - ly;

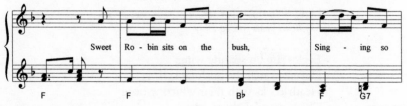

Sweet Ro - bin sits on the bush, Sing - ing so

rare - ly,___ "Tell me thou bon - nie bird, When shall I

mar - ry me?" "When six braw gen - tle - men Kirk - ward shall car - ry ye."

"Tell me, thou bonnie bird,
When shall I marry me?"
"When six braw gentlemen
Kirkward shall carry ye."

"Who makes the bridal bed?
Birdie, say truly."
"The grey-headed sexton
That delves the grave duly.

The glow-worm o'er grave and stone
Shall light thee steady.
The owl from the steeple sing
"Welcome, proud lady.'"

Sir Walter Scott

Rest My Ain Bairnie

O___ rest my ain bair-nie, lie peace-ful and still;___

Emin   Emin   B   Emin

Sleep - ing or wak - ing I'll guard thee from ill!

G Amin D   D   G   D   A   D

Fair be thy bo - dy, far whi - ter than snow,

Emin   Emin   G   D

No e - vil mark from the heel to the brow.

B♭   C   B♭   Emin

Eerily gathers the mist on Ben Shee,
Coldly the wind sweeps in from the sea,
But terror and storm may come east or come west,
Warm will my birdie bide in the nest.

Then rest, my ain bairnie, lie peaceful and still,
Sleeping or waking I'll guard thee from ill

Fresh as the heather thy boyhood will bloom,
Strong as the pine thy manhood will come,
Flower of thy kinsmen, chief of thy clan,
King of my heart, thou bonnie wee man.

Then rest, my ain bairnie, lie peaceful and still,
Sleeping or waking I'll guard thee from ill

Harold Boulton

Rise and Follow Charlie

Sound the pi-broch loud on high, Frae John o' Groats to Isle of Skye; Let a' the clans their slo-gan cry, And rise and fol-low Char - lie.

Tha tighin fodham, fodh - am, fodh - am, tha tighin fodh - am, fodh-am, fodh-am,

Tha tighin fodham, fodh-am, fodham, tha tighin fodh - am eir - igh.

And see a small devoted band
By dark Loch Shiel have ta'en their stand,
And proudly vow with heart and hand
To fight for royal Charlie.

Tha tighin fodham, fodham, fodham,
Tha tighin fodham, fodham, fodham,
Tha tighin fodham, fodham, fodham,
Tha tighin fodham, eirigh!

From every hill and every glen
Are gathering fast the loyal men,
They grasp their dirks and shout again
"Hurrah! for royal Charlie!"

Tha tighin fodham, fodham, fodham,
Tha tighin fodham, fodham, fodham,
Tha tighin fodham, fodham, fodham,
Tha tighin fodham, eirigh!

On dark Culloden's field of gore
Hark! Hark! they shout "Claymore! claymore!"
They bravely fight, what can they more?
They die for royal Charlie.

Tha tighin fodham, fodham, fodham,
Tha tighin fodham, fodham, fodham,
Tha tighin fodham, fodham, fodham,
Tha tighin fodham, eirigh!

No more we'll see such deeds again,
Deserted is each Highland glen,

And lonely cairns are o'er the men
Who fought and died for Charlie.

Tha tighin fodham, fodham, fodham,
Tha tighin fodham, fodham, fodham,
Tha tighin fodham, fodham, fodham,
Tha tighin fodham, eirigh!

Mrs Norman MacLeod (Senior)

The Rowan Tree

Oh!— Row-an Tree, Oh! Row-an Tree! thou'lt aye be dear to me,— En-twin'd thou art wi' mo-ny ties, o' hame and in-fan-cy. Thy leaves were aye the first o' spring, Thy flow'rs the sim-mer's pride; There was nae sic a bon-ny tree in a' the coun-trie-side. Oh!— Row-an Tree.

How fair wert thou in simmer time, wi' a' thy clusters white,
How rich and gay thy autumn dress, wi' berries red and bright.
On thy fair stem were many names, which now nae mair I see,
But they're engraven on my heart; forgot they ne'er can be.
Oh! Rowan Tree.

We sat aneath thy spreading shade, the bairnies round thee ran;
They pu'd thy bonny berries red, and necklaces they strang.
My mother! Oh, I see her yet, she smiled oor sports to see,
Wi' little Jeanie on her lap, and Jamie at her knee.
Oh! Rowan Tree.

Oh, there arose my father's prayer, in holy evening's calm;
How sweet was then my mother's voice, in the Martyr's psalm.
Now a' are gane. We meet nae mair, aneath the Rowan tree;
But hallowed thoughts around thee twine, o' hame and infancy.
Oh! Rowan Tree.

Scotland the Brave

Hark when the night is fall-ing, Hear! hear the pipes are call-ing,

D

Loud - ly and proud-ly call-ing, down thro' the glen.

G   D   E7   A sus4 A

There where the hills are sleep- ing, Now feel the blood a - leap-ing,

D

High as the spi - rits of the old High - land men.

G   D   G   D

Chorus

Tower - ing in gal - lant fame, Scot - land my moun-tain hame,

A   A7   D   G   D

High may your proud stand-ards glo-ri-ous-ly wave.

Land of my high en-deav-our, Land of the shin-ing ri-ver,

Land of my heart for-e-ver, Scot-land the brave.

High in the misty Highlands,
Out by the purple islands,
Brave are the hearts that beat beneath Scottish skies;
Wild are the winds that greet you,
Staunch are the friends that meet you,
Kind as the light that shines from fair maidens' eyes.

Towering in gallant fame,
Scotland, my mountain hame,
High may your proud standards gloriously wave.
Land of my high endeavour,
Land of the shining river,
Land of my heart forever,
Scotland the brave.

Cliff Hanley

The Skye Boat Song

Speed bonnie boat, like a bird on the wing,
Onward, the sailor's cry;
Carry the lad that's born to be king,
Over the sea to Skye.

Though the waves leap, soft shall ye sleep;
Ocean's a royal bed.
Rocked on the deep, Flora will keep
Watch by your weary head.

Speed bonnie boat, etc.

Many's the lad fought on that day,
Well the claymore could wield:
When the night came, silently lay
Dead on Culloden field.

Speed bonnie boat, etc.

Burned are our homes, exile and death
Scatter the loyal men;
Yet ere the sword cool in the sheath,
Charlie will come again.

Speed bonnie boat, etc.

Harold Boulton

Sugar Candy

There was a wee las-sie aw-fy thin, A bun-dle o' bones wrapped up in skin, Now she's get-tin' a wee dou-ble chin, Wi' eat-in' su-gar can - dy.

Chorus

Al - ly bal - ly, al - ly bal - ly bee, sit - tin' on your mam - my's knee, Greet - in' for a - no-ther baw - bee To buy some su - gar can - dy.

Puir wee Johnnie's greetin' too:
What can his puir mammy do,
But gi'e them a penny atween them two,
To buy some sugar candy.

Ally bally, ally bally bee,
Sittin' on your mammy's knee,
Greetin' for another bawbee,
To buy some sugar candy.

Here's a penny, ma bonnie wee man,
Rin doon the road as fast as ye can,
Dinna stop till Coulter's van,
An' buy some sugar candy.

Ally bally, etc.

This is No My Plaid

My plaid was silken, saft and warm,
It wrapt me round frae arm to arm,
And like himsel' it had a charm,
And O! my plaid was dear to me.
But this is no my plaid, my plaid, my plaid,
This is no my plaid, bonnie though the colours be.

The lad that gied 't me lo'ed me weel,
He lo'ed me maist as weel's himsel',
And though his name I daurna tell,
Yet o' my plaid is dear to me.
But this is no my plaid, my plaid, my plaid,
This is no my plaid, bonnie though the colours be.

W Haley

Turn Ye to Me

The waves are dancing merrily, merrily,
Ho ro Mhairi dhu, turn ye to me;
The sea-birds are wailing wearily, wearily,
Ho ro Mhairi dhu, turn ye to me.
Hushed be thy moaning, lone bird of the sea,
Thy home on the rocks is a shelter to thee,
Thy home is the angry wave,
Mine but the lonely grave,
Ho ro Mhairi dhu, turn ye to me.

John Wilson *("Christopher North")*

The Twa Corbies

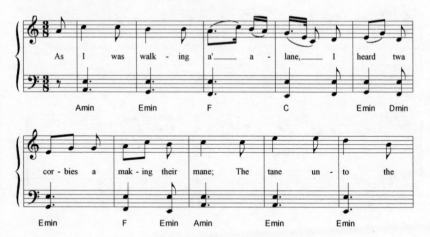

As I was walk - ing a'___ a - lane,___ I heard twa

Amin   Emin   F   C   Emin Dmin

cor - bies a mak - ing their mane; The tane un - to the

Emin   F   Emin Amin   Emin   Emin

ti - ther did say,___ Whaur sall___ we gang___ and dine the day?

Amin   C   Emin Amin Emin Dmin   Dmin Emin Amin

"In behint yon auld fail dyke
I wot there lies a new-slain knight;
And naebody kens that he lies there
But his hawk and his hound and his lady fair."

"His hound is to the huntin' gane,
His hawk to fetch the wild-fowl hame,
His lady's ta'en anither mate,
Sae we may mak' our dinner sweet."

"Ye'll sit on his white hause-bane,
And I'll pike out his bonnie blue e'en;
Wi' ae lock o' his gowden hair
We'll theek our nest whar it grows bare."

"Mony's the ane for him mak's mane,
But nane sall ken whar he is gane;
Owre his white banes, when they are bare,
The wind sall blaw for evermair."

Old Scottish Song

The Uist Tramping Song

Chorus

Come a - long, come a - long, Let us foot it out to - ge - ther; Come a -

long, come a - long, Be it fair or storm - y wea - ther, With the

hills of home be - fore us And the pur - ple of the hea - ther, Let us

sing in hap - py cho - rus, Come a - long, come a - long. So—

Verse

gai - ly sings the lark, And the sky's all a - wake With the

pro - mise of the day, For the road we glad - ly take; So it's

heel and toe and for - ward, Bid - ding fare - well to the town,___ For the

wel - come that a - waits us Ere the sun goes down.

Come along, come along,
Let us foot it out together;
Come along, come along,
Be it fair or stormy weather,
With the hills of home before us
And the purple of the heather,
Let us sing in happy chorus,
Come along, come along.

It's the call of sea and shore,
It's the tang of bog and peat,
And the scent of brier and myrtle
That puts magic in our feet;
So it's on we go, rejoicing,
Over bracken, over style;
And it's soon we will be tramping
Out the last, long mile.

Come along, etc.

Hugh Roberton,
from the Gaelic of
Archibald MacDonald

Wae's Me for Prince Charlie

A wee bird cam' to our ha' door, He warbled sweet and clearly, And aye the o'er come o' his sang, Was "Wae's me for Prince Charlie." Oh! when I heard the bonnie, bonnie bird, The tears came drappin' rarely: I took my bonnet aff my head For weel I lo'ed Prince Charlie.

Quo' I, "My bird, my bonnie, bonnie bird,
Is that a tale ye borrow?
Or is't some words ye've learned by rote
Frae a lilt o' dule and sorrow?"
"Oh, no, no, no," the wee bird sang,
"I've flown sin' morning early,
On sic a day o' wind and rain –
Oh, wae's me for Prince Charlie!

"On hills that are by rights his ain
He roves, a lonely stranger;
On ilka hand he's pressed by want;
On ilka side by danger.
Yestreen I saw him in a glen;
My heart near bursted fairly,
For sairly changed by want was he –
Oh, wae's me for Prince Charlie!

"Dark night cam' on, and tempest howl'd
Loud ower the muirs and valleys;
And where was it your Prince lay down,
Wha's hame should been a palace?
He row'd him in a Hieland plaid
That cover'd him but sparely,
And slept beneath a bush o' broom –
"Oh, wae's me for Prince Charlie!"

But now the bird saw some red-coats,
And shook his wings wi' anger.
Cried he, "This land is no for me:
I'll tarry here nae langer."
A while he hovered, on the wing,
Ere he departed fairly,
But aye the o'ercome o' his sang
Was "Wae's me for Prince Charlie!"

Weaving Song

Gae owre the muir, gae doun the brae, Gae busk my bower to mak' it rea-dy; For

I'm gaun there to wed the day, The bon-nie lad that wears the plai-die.

Twine weel the bon-nie tweel, Twist weel the plai - die, For

O! I lo'e the lad - die weel, That wears the tar - tan plai - die.

Content his lowly cot I'll share,
I ask nae mair to mak' life cheerie;
Wi' heart sae leal and love sae true
The langest day can ne'er seem eerie.

Twine weel the bonnie tweel,
Twist weel the plaidie,
For O! I lo'e the laddie weel
That wears the tartan plaidie.

Weel sheltered in his Hieland plaid
Frae worldly cares I'll aye be easy;
Its storms I'll hear like blasts that blaw
Owre heather bell and mountain daisy.

Twine weel, etc.

Scottish Song

The Wee Cooper o' Fife

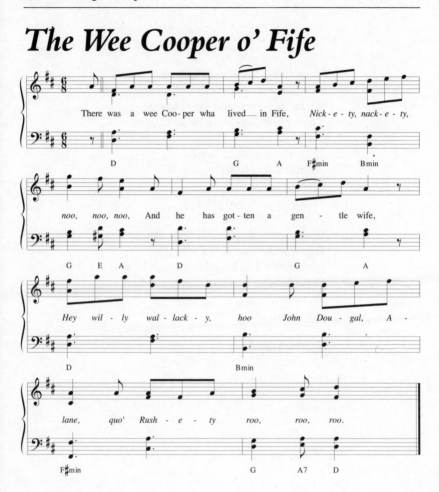

There was a wee Coo-per wha lived— in Fife, *Nick - e - ty, nack - e - ty,*

noo, noo, noo, And he has got - ten a gen - tle wife,

Hey wil - ly wal - lack - y, hoo John Dou - gal, A -

lane, quo' Rush - e - ty roo, roo, roo.

She wadna bake, and she wadna brew,
Nickety, nackety, noo noo noo,
For spoilin' o' her comely hue;
Hey willy wallacky, hoo John Dougal,
Alane, quo' Rushety, roo roo roo.

She wadna card, and she wadna spin,
Nickety, nackety, etc.
For thinkin' o' her gentle kin;
Hey willy wallacky, etc.

The cooper has gone to his wool-pack,
Nickety, nackety, etc.
And laid a sheep-skin on his wife's back;
Hey willy wallacky, etc.

I'll no thrash ye, for your gentle kin,
Nickety nackety, etc.
But I will thrash my ain sheep-skin.
Hey willy wallacky, etc.

Oh, I will bake and I will brew,
Nickety, nackety, etc.
And think nae mair on my comely hue;
Hey, willy wallacky, etc.

Oh, I will card, and I will spin,
Nickety, nackety, etc.
And think nae mair on my gentle kin;
Hey willy wallacky, etc.

All ye wha hae gotten a gentle wife,
Nickety, nackety, etc.
Just think ye on the wee cooper o' Fife,
Hey, willy wallacky, etc.

We Will Take the Good Old Way

Up the steep and heathery ben,
Doun the bonnie winding glen,
We march, a band of loyal men,
Let them say their will, O!

*We will take the good old way, we will take the good old way,
We'll take and keep the good old way, let them say their will,
    O!*

We will march adoun Glencoe,
We will march adoun Glencoe,
By the ferry we will go,
Let them say their will, O!

We will take, etc.

To Glengarry and Lochiel,
Loyal hearts, with arms of steel,
These will back you in the field,
Let them say their will, O!

We will take, etc.

Cluny will come doun the brae,
Keppoch bold will lead the way,
Toss thine antlers, Caber Feidh,
Let them say their will, O!

We will take, etc.

Forward, sons of bold Rob Roy,
Stewarts' conflict is your joy
We'll stand together pour le Roy,
Let them say their will, O!

We will take, etc.

**Translated from the Gaelic by
the Rev A Stewart, LLD**

When the Kye Come Hame

Come, all ye jol - ly shep - herds, That whis - tle through the glen, I'll

tell ye o' a se - cret that cour - tiers din - na ken. What is the great - est bliss that the

tongue o' man can name 'Tis to woo a bon - nie lass - ie When the

kye come hame, When the kye come hame, When the kye come hame, 'Tween the

gloam - in' and the mirk, When the kye come hame.

'Tis not beneath the burgonet
Nor yet beneath the crown,
'Tis not on couch of velvet
Nor yet on bed of down;
'Tis beneath the spreading birch
In the dell without a name,
Wi' a bonnie, bonnie lassie
When the kye come hame.

Awa' wi' fame and fortune:
What comforts can they gi'e?
And a' the arts that prey upon
Man's life and liberty!
Gi'e me the highest joy
That the heart o' man can frame:
My bonnie, bonnie lassie
When the kye come hame.

James Hogg

Willie's Gane to Melville Castle

O Wil-lie's gane to Mel-ville Cas-tle, Boots and spurs an' a', To bid the led-dies a' fare-weel Be-fore he ga'ed a-wa'. Wil-lie's young and blithe and bon-nie, Lo'ed by ane an' a', Oh! what will all the las-ses do When Wil-lie gaes a-wa'?

The first he met was Lady Kate,
She led him through the ha',
And wi' a sad and sorry heart
She loot the tear-drop fa'.
Beside the fire stood Lady Grace,
Said ne'er a word ava;
She thocht that she was sure o' him
Before he gaed awa'.

Then ben the house cam' Lady Bell,
"Gude troth ye need na craw,
Maybe the lad will fancy me,
And disappoint ye a'."
Doun the stair tripped Lady Jean,
The flower amang them a',
"O lasses trust in Providence
An' ye'll get husbands a'."

When on his horse he rade awa'
They gathered round the door,
He gaily waved his bonnet blue,
They set up sic a roar,
Their cries, their tears brocht Willie back,
He kissed them ane an' a',
"O lasses bide till I come hame
And then I'll wed ye a'."

Old Scottish Ballad

Wi' a Hundred Pipers

hun - dred pi - pers an' a', an' a', wi' a hun - dred pi - pers an'

a', an' a', We'll up an' gie them a blaw, a blaw, Wi' a

hun - dred pi - pers an' a', an' a'.

Oh, our sodger lads look'd braw, look'd braw,
Wi' their tartan kilts, and a' and a'
Wi' bonnets, feathers and glitterin' gear,
An' pibrochs soundin' sweet and clear.
Will they a' return to their ain dear glen?
Will they a' return, oor Hieland men?
Second-sichted Sandy look'd fu' wae,
And mithers grat as they marched away.

Wi' a hundred pipers an' a', an' a',
Wi' a hundred pipers an' a', an' a',
We'll up an' gie them a blaw, a blaw,
Wi' a hundred pipers an' a', an' a'.

Oh, wha is foremost of a', of a'?
Oh, wha does follow the blaw, the blaw?
Bonnie Charlie, the Prince o' us a', hurrah!
Wi' his hundred pipers, and a', and a'.
His bonnet and feathers he's wavin' high,
His prancin' steed just seems to fly,
The nor' wind sweeps thro' his golden hair,
An' the pibrochs blaw wi' an unco flare.

Wi' a hundred pipers etc.

Lady Nairne

Ye Banks and Braes o' Bonnie Doon

Oft ha'e I roved by bonnie Doon
To see the rose and woodbine twine;
And ilka bird sang o' its love,
And fondly sae did I o' mine.
Wi' lightsome heart I pu'd a rose,
Fu' sweet upon its thorny tree:
But my fause lover stole my rose,
But Ah! he left the thorn wi' me.

Robert Burns

Glossary

a' all
aboon above
afore before
aftimes often, oftentimes
agam (Gaelic) signifies possession (e.g. Geordie agam = my Geordie)
ain own
amang among
ance once
ane one
aneath underneath, beneath
aught anything.
auld lang syne days of long ago
auld old
awa away
aye always, still
bags bagpipes
bairn, bairnie baby, child
baith both
bawbee small coin, half-penny.
behint behind
ben 1 mountain or hill **2** through, in (e.g. into a room)

bheag little (Gaelic)
bigg build
birk birch
birken of birches
blaw blow
bleer blur
blin' blind
bogle apparition.
bonnie pretty
bothy wooden hut or little cottage
boun' bound
brae slope
braid broad
braw fine, handsome.
brig, brigg bridge
brocht brought
brunt burnt.
burd lady, damsel.
burgonet knightly helmet.
burn stream
burnie small stream
burnside riverbank
busk prepare
but and ben two-roomed house
ca' call
cailzie-cock capercaillie or

capercailzie. A wood grouse or mountain cock

caller fresh

can'le candle

canach cotton grass (Gaelic)

canna cannot

canny cautious, prudent

canty happy

cauf calf

cauld cold

cheerie happy

chevalier a favourite son

chiel fellow, lad, chap

claymore sword

coft bought

cooper maker or repairer of casks

corbie raven or hooded crow

coronach dirge or lament

craw crow, boast

creel fish basket

croodlin cooing

croon sing

cruit mo chridh dear harp of mine (Gaelic)

cushie, cushat pigeon, dove

dalicht daylight

daunce dance

daurna dare not

dee die

deil devil

dirk dagger

dochter daughter

dool sadness

douce amiable, quiet, sedate

doun down

dowf useless

driech drab

dule sad fate

Dunedin Edinburgh

duniwassal, dunie-wassal follower of a Highland chief

dwine pine, wane

dwining pining, waning

dyke wall

e'e eye

e'en eyes

eerie afraid

enueuch enough

erst in the first place

fa fall

fail-dyke a field wall built with sods of earth

faither father
fareweel farewell
farin fare
fause false
fecht fight
fecht fight
fee to be hired
fere companion
fit foot
forbye over and above
frae from
froon frown
gae go
gait, gate way; conduct
gane gone
gang go
gart made
gear goods
gear possessions
ghaist ghost
gie give
gien given
gin until, if, should
glen valley, dale
gloamin' twilight.
Gow Niel Gow, the violinist, composer of the original tune
gowan daisy

gowd gold.
gowden golden
grat cried, wept
greet weep
greetin crying
gude good
guid good
hairst harvest.
hairst harvest
halesome wholesome
hame home
hame home
han' hand
hause-bane collar bone
heeze hoist up
hielands highlands
hirsel flock
holm river bank
hose, hosen, hoshen stockings
ilk, ilka each, every.
ither other
jeer brag, proclaim.
jo dear one
jorum bottle, punch-bowl.
kent knew
kirk church
kirkward towards the church

knowe knoll
kye cows
lanely lonely
lang long
lave rest, remainder
lawland lowland
lawlands lowands
lea field of unfurrowed
grass
leal true,
leal chaste, loyal, honest
lea-rig strip of grass left
unploughed in a fur-
rowed field
lee-lang long
leeze me, leese me is dear
to me
leeze, leese, leis
be lease to
leglin milk-pail.
licht light
lichtly lightly
lo'e love
loon young man
loot let
loot let
lown still, peaceful
lyart grey
maist most

mammy mother
mane mourn, lament
maun must
maunna must not
mavis song thrush
mayna may not
mear mare
Menie form of Marian
mettled sturdy
mickle, muckle much
minnie mother
mirk dark
mirkest darkest
mither mother
mo nighean dhu
my dark-haired maid
mony many
muir moor
naethin nothing
nane none
neebour neighbour
neist next
nocht nothing
noo now
nought nothing
owre over
owse ox
owsen oxen
paidl't paddled

pair pair of horses
pearlies tears
pelisses palaces
philabeg kilt
pibroch pipe music.
pike pick
pint-stoup two-quart measure
plaid Highland outer dress
prentice apprentice
puir poor
rade rode
rade rode
rin run
rokley, rokelay short cloak
row wrap
rows flows
sae so
sall shall
saul, saule soul
saut salt, salty
scrunt a stump or stalk, anything worn down
shae shoe
shaw grove
shieling cottage
shoon shod
shoon shoes
sian a pile of grass (Gaelic)

sic such
simmer summer
sklent slope
snaw snow
snotter candle wax, snot from the nose
socht sought
sodger soldier
spak spoke
stu mo run joy of my heart (Gaelic)
sughin streaming past
swain young man
swaird sward
tak take
tak take
tane unto the tither one to the other
tapsalteerie topsy-turvy.
tent pay attention.
tentless careless
theek thatch
thocht thought
tine lose
tine, tyne perish, lose, miss
toun town
trepan pierce
Turra Turriff
twa two

tweel twill, diagonally-crossed cloth

twine spin, twist

twiner one who twisted spun yarn into thicker threads

unco remarkable

wad would

wae woe

wae woe

waefu' woeful

wan won

wardly worldly

wark work; building; business; trouble, fuss, outcry

warld world

warldlings worldly people

waukin awakening

wean child

wede awa(y) carried away, removed

weel well

weir war

whar, whaur where

whin, whinne sharp rock; prickly bush such as gorse

willie-waucht powerful swig

wime belly

yestreen yesterday evening

yett gate; a pass between mountains

yon that

yowes sheep, ewes

Other titles in this series published by
Waverley Books

A History of Scotland

A Scottish Miscellany

Scottish Ghosts

Scottish Jokes

Scottish Murders

Scottish Myths & Legends

Scottish Names

Scottish Place Names

Scottish Witches

Traditional Scottish Recipes

150 Famous Scots